Rag Trade

Miriam Sagan

Rag Trade

P O E M S

La Alameda Press   ::   Albuquerque

These poems first appeared in the following publications:
"Fabric" in *Poetica*; "Prayer Flag" in the chapbook *Future Tense
of Ash* (Modest Proposal/Lilliput); "New Jersey Book of the Dead,"
"Attack of the Killer Husbands," "Florida: The Water Bird,"
"Translating Catullus," "Anxiety," "Bridge of Discontinuity,"
"Spiral Hill," appeared in the e-zine *Santa Fe Poetry Broadside;*
"Internment Camp," "Black Ollas," in *Heaven Bone*; "Refugees"
in the e-zine *Big Bridge;* "Artichoke Heart" in *The Eldorado Sun*
and *Written with a Spoon* (Sherman Asher); "Things I Have Eaten"
in *Chiron Review;* "Aristotle" in the e-zine *Stirring;* "Plato's Cave"
in *The George Washington Review;* "Keys" and "Hatched" in
Front Range Review; "Fairy Tale" in *Puerta del Sol;* "Nude with
a Gas Mask," "You Ate Phil Whalen's Noodles," "Petrified Forest,"
"Measuring the Moon," "Going East in West Texas" in the e-zine
Muse Apprentice; "Brautigan" in *Rio Grande Review;* "A Fever,"
"Choreographer," in the e-zine *Facets;* "Good Girls" in *Staple Gun;*
Sections of "Counting the Omer" in *Water Blossoms; Kokako;
Paper Wasp; Nightingale;* "San Luis" in the e-zine *Eye/Optic.*

Thanks to the Lannan Foundation for the Marfa residency grant,
during which many of these poems were written.
And to Miriam Bobkoff for her help with this manuscript.

Front Cover: VINTAGE CURTAIN MATERIAL / collection of the publisher
Back Cover: CHINESE SILK EMBROIDERY / collection of the author

Library of Congress Cataloging-in-Publication Data

Sagan, Miriam, 1954-
  Rag trade : poems / Miriam Sagan.
  p. cm.
  ISBN 1-888809-42-6 (alk. paper)
  I. Title.
PS3569.A288R34 2004
811'.54—dc22

                                        2004000982

La Alameda Press
9636 Guadalupe Trail NW
Albuquerque, New Mexico 87114

Contents

Gypsy Hand

Just below street level, the little door
With the oval windows obscured
By pasted fabric, white cotton with black moons
Rusted doorknob and for a knocker
White plaster hand centered
Palm down. I don't descend
Three small steps
Although I want
To know who lives here
Who cut up the Indian print skirt
To cover the glass
And now goes naked, half-undressed,
Who placed the romantic antique-looking
Hand with the long tapered fingers
Above the doorknob too rusted to turn.
Rush of spring air like a song
I'd heard before, then forgotten
What is this sound of the sea
I hear in my left ear
A thousand miles from any bay?
Why do I suddenly tremble
As if reminded of a love
Both old and new?
Why do I taste the iron
Of blood in my mouth
As if from a lip split by kissing
Or a harsh pomegranate?
Because what I say is true.

Ikat

Try starting here—
An overcast afternoon with snow,
Sky covered with a Two Grey Hills blanket
As if across a bee-hive shaped door.
Entering the concert hall
Strains of Mahler surround
Settings of Chinese poems
Words translated for export
Like blue floral porcelain
Manufactured for trade,
A usual phrase—
"Autumn twilight," "Bridge of jade."
Ideogram as decorative design
Not the harsh direct dialect of the archaic, still
As I sit in the medium-expensive seat
The music is exquisite
Particularly at the end
Where the singer pauses
Until the strings pick up the voice
Across a void of silence
For the composer whose child is dead,
Whose own heart is weak.
Music tugs at feeling
Despite the requisite moonlight
Reflected in the lake of the poem
As if there were another world than this . . .
Our own moon
One day past full

Rising in bare cottonwood branches
Last night filled the kitchen window
Over the unwashed dishes.

Trade was everything
To the Jews of the Silk Route
Pushed from Persia
To the dry back end of the world
Bukhara, Samarkand
Cities that once welcomed kings.
Now Jews live with Tajiks who worship fire
Until some pious rabbi removes
Persian holidays from the holy calendar.
Here, they must dye and weave
Walled gardens of ikat on silk velour.
Jewish women without chador
Can dance steps from before the Ottomans came
Treading a path as intricate as thread
Rose on violet silk, color of desert far-off.
Tajiks control the yellow and the red.
For ocean, sky, for indigo, for blue
The weaver must "go to the Jew"
For cold dyed fabric
Color like an infinite
Expanse of longing, restlessness.

Jews must wear wool or cotton
In the presence of a Muslim,
Wear silk at home,
Gold tinkling bracelets of seclusion
Like a walled city, like Queen Esther
At home in exile.

The dyer's hand is permanently stained
Like handprints of pre-history
On desert rock outcroppings;
Despised more than garbage collectors
Or those who haul dead animals to ditches,
Forbidden the communal eating dish
Stain of beauty, taboo, transformative.

Ikat, as a word, comes from Indonesia
As a technique, from China
There is no metaphor
In bound and bundled thread
It's not like life,
Being able to see ahead
From the resistance dyed cluster
To the entire.
Whatever happened in the Jurassic
Was not intended
To pave the floor of the Denver Public Library—
Fossils of ammonite like a chambered nautilus,
Belemnite like bullet-shaped squid or octopus,
Slabs quarried where Romans hewed stone
Transported here, where tourists stand and stare
Ask directions to the capital's mile-high step
Or search for something in a book
A phrase remembered, a twist of plot,
Believing, as all readers do,
They can reclaim the lost.
Empires recede, warm oceans from the shore
And we are left cast up
In dry desert town at break of day.

The caravans have gone away
To east, to west, burdened with their tinkling bells.
Stone Buddhas blasted
Out of their standing caves
By terrible regime,
Biggest standing Buddha in the world
No longer steps forward.
It's strange to eventually realize
The Greek marble girl
Engraved on a stele, holding a white dove
Is the funeral marker for a dead child.
If you could understand,
If you could step from cliff to cloud
Or float like raven in updraft of air
Or fasten with a clasp of jade
The cloak the Bodhisattva wears—
The Bodhisattva, she will come on down
To bars and pawn shops at the end of town,
Listen to that far-off whistle of the train.

Honey

I went to buy honey on Oñate Street.
Last time I had been there
Gate was locked,
Too early, or too late—
Behind the wooden fence a buzzing sound.
Yes, I'd seen them all over the neighborhood
Buzzing in autumn's chamisa,
Spring's white flowered pyracantha,
That firethorn that stings like hornets.
But this Friday in May, luck held,
A sign reading HONEY had appeared
Over the gate and we went in.

My twelve year old daughter was home
Sick from school
With a sore throat.
As we entered the yard
Full of hives
They looked not so much like dresser drawers
But stacked up like the coffins of children
During some war or terrible epidemic.
Bees were everywhere, and my daughter
Suddenly seemed much younger
As if she might take my hand.
I'd been hearing from the neighbors about the honey man—
I told my husband: I'm going to the honey man.
And he began to sing:
Oh baby, stay here with me

Don't go to the honey man!
But today it was a woman
Behind the table, standing and selling
An array of honey
Talking to a woman with a large cross
Buying honey for the Russian orthodox church.
The honey man's wife was named Irina
Slavic accent, a pretty flustered look
Making change as if she only spoke
The language of bees.
On a whim, at home, I looked her up—
Saint Irina, tortured by kings
Balkan, or a Slav,
Drowned with a millstone
Until water flowed back
The stream turned away from her
And she was saved.
The sword broke as it aimed at her neck,
Earthquake opened the ground,
Swallowed her tormentors.
Her inviolate virtue
Repels all assault.
To my shock I also discover
Today, May 18th
Is St. Irina's feast day.

"Honey is good for your throat," Irina
Tells my daughter
Offering us different tastes on little sticks,
Taste of dandelion high meadow blossom,
Dark, light, we swallow it.
Honey can dress a wound

Even a wound that will not heal,
Soothe sunburn, scrape, prolong life
According to the Greek physician Hippocrates.

Beehive tombs of Mycenae,
Kazanlak's valley of the tombs,
Thracian horses race across Bulgaria,
Tombs of brick rise against a barren mountain range,
A sacrifice of chariots, horses, slaves
Mars the ante-chambers of Asia Minor,
Even the Etruscans kept bees.

Much farther back, the bees emerge
As dinosaurs cease to walk the earth.
Honey before there is a noun to say it
Before the hunters with their verbs.
For yes, it is a bee preserved in amber,
Something ancient which implies the flower
A forest of birch trees
Pollinating wind.
These beehives look like a line of rural mailboxes
Where mellifluous messages arrive.
My daughter and I each pick one jar of honey
Carry home the load
Where they will sit glowing in the kitchen
Like two beautiful women—
One dark, one gold.

Fabric

Because the light of creation is hidden
                    within the form of creation
Cloth covers the braided challah,
Cross-stitched tablecloth
Covers the table,
There is a curtain for the Torah ark,
Mantle for the scroll,
Cover for the reader's desk
Red silk embroidered with metallic thread.

To beautify creation
With needle and thread
With thimble and pinprick
With Spanish work:
Gold and silver threads
Woven into a braid
Stitched to a pattern—
Lost in the wind . . .

613 fringes on the prayer shawl
613 commandments
613 seeds in a pomegranate
Dowry cloth from Bukhara
Undyed linen
Florettes in circles in multi-colored silk
Curtain from partitioned Poland
The wedding canopy itself

As if the world were veiled like a bride
Were draped in purdah
As if she might be anyone, veiled girl
As Jacob found
The wrong sister beneath her curtain of hair
Became a man with two wives
A man with two selves, one of which will wrestle
The other to the ground . . .

Prayer Flag

Wood is not the past tense of fire,
The future of fire is not ash,
Someone or other gave us this green prayer flag
And we forgot all about it in the hall closet.
Luck is not the past tense of water wheel
Although Genghis Khan may be the future tense of city,
Nomad is the past tense of Jew,
A word with the future tense messiah.
The pottery army stands firm in the ground
Guarding the tomb of the long dead king
Six thousand life size figures
Stare forward into nothing.
The archeologist is still just a girl
With her hair caught in a pink chiffon scarf
Her hands hold a brush, minister delicately
To the mute remnant of impossible desire.
At the great tomb on the Silk Road,
Who cut off the hands and heads
Of every figure of an ambassador
Carved along the avenue?
The past tense of Marco Polo is Italy,
My present tense is full of potted geraniums,
The prayer flag hangs from the portal
Over the woodpile and the Mexican sunflowers.
Wind that doesn't stop day or night
Raises the green lotus in the air.
The past tense of oasis is water,
The future tense of oasis is sand,

Even pottery tokens stamped with the Buddha
Lie exposed like pebbles on the tide of the desert.
This prayer flag comes from Lama mountain
Actually, there is no wind at all
The air is still, it is the flag that is moving.
The past tense of fire is fire
The future tense of ash is ash
A pink rosebush climbs the front wall of our house—
Look, it's just about to bloom.

New Jersey Book of the Dead

The rest stops on the New Jersey turnpike
Are named for poets—
Walt Whitman, William Carlos Williams, but no
Allen Ginsberg, or Allen Ginsberg's father.
Still, I often dream
I've been left behind
At the Joyce Kilmer rest stop—
I'm not wearing shoes
Stand on grunge in my stocking feet
And the bus has left—
An ambiguous dream bus
That might mean more than one thing
Or two things at once
Or nothing at all—
Bus full of protesters against the war
Headed south to Washington, D.C.
Or a psychedelically painted hippie bus
Going to Haight Ashbury without me
Or not a bus at all, but a sedan
Oldsmobile with my father, mother, sisters, brother
Generic family
That still leaves me behind.

As a child, you searched for the alluvial—
Marsh, swamp, what lies beneath
The highway bridge, beyond the cul-de-sac
Over the concrete culvert, under the wire.
There was a pond there, in the middle of woods,

You waded in
Waist deep,
Covered in mud,
Spent hours
Trying to catch the snake.
The snake was black, thicker than your boyish wrist,
It snapped, and tried to bite.
And although you usually excelled
At catching things that did not want to be caught
Even with a stick
You could not catch this snake,
Went home wet to dinner.
It was only hours later, looking in a book
That you realized
It was a water moccasin,
Deadly poisonous
Shocked even your ten-year old self
At how close you'd come to death.

This was a world where babies were snatched
From peaceful bassinets—
You could be alive and warm one moment,
Then kidnapped the next, hit by a car,
Bitten by a snake, stung by a yellow jacket,
Suffocated in a closet, smothered in a dry cleaning bag,
Locked in an abandoned refrigerator.
On purpose, or by mistake, the litany went on
Scared me out of the skin I'd been born with
Into some other kind of carapace.
When the police pulled me over
It took every ounce of strength I had in my body
Not to leap out of the car

And start running away across the neighborhood
Jumping fences, crashing through hedges.
Escape was hard-wired into my cells.
As a middle-aged woman
Thousands of miles from New Jersey
I could barely wait in the car
For the simple traffic citation
Of failing to signal. No, this was the escape
From East Berlin, or Nazis, a noir film
Or just my belief
That the cops would as soon
Shoot as look at me.

Maybe it is because of the drug dealers—
The way everyone trafficked
In controlled substances—
From phisohex to ludes to love.
Girls in white lipstick dealt so much
I was sure they would end up dead in a ditch
But instead they became public defenders
For the state of New Jersey.
There was your friend, that really heavy dealer
Who became an anesthesiologist—
That guy, we always said,
Loved knocking people out for money.
But what about that other dealer,
The one who got so paranoid
He thought airplanes and helicopters
Were following him personally—
There was one light in the sky
In particular
That followed him unrelentingly.

It took him months to realize—
It was the north star.

The holy say
Everything is interconnected
And that's not only true, but good.
Where I grew up
We believed everything was connected
But out to get us.
One of my best friends
Taught me to smoke and play poker
On the off chance, she emphasized
That I was captured by a motorcycle gang
And needed these social skills.
You talkin' to me? Are you talking to me?
Do you know what I require?
I hold what beats the Queen of Hearts, the Ace of Spades—
Desire.

I Went Looking for Myself Someplace Else

The large photograph on the museum wall
Shows the widows of Mozambique
Heads thrown back, arms outstretched
Refugees preparing to return.
Widows, the caption says, who must
Exorcize their husbands' ghosts
Soldiers who fell in battle—
Tribal, internecine,
People who will kill
For the wrong language, phrase, a turn
Of custom, or the name of God.

These widows burn the small houses
They've lived in for years
To show they are leaving, once and for all,
This land of exile.
Certainly they'll take their children
Their pots and pans
Home, but leave
The spirits of the divisive dead behind.

I read about Afghanistan—
The widow who will drop
A grenade on the Taliban
From the flat roof of her adobe compound.
Who among us
Doesn't want some kind of revenge?

Although you'd think I'd be over it
By now, years after your death.
Still I go seeking
For comparisons extreme and violent
To what I felt
I also would have liked
To drop a grenade,
Burn a house,
Deride death—that vehicle
Of loss.

Internment Camp

It slips from the envelope
Copy of a photograph—
Three rows,
Internees at a Justice Department
Detention camp. It was this
Exact neighborhood
Along the Alameda and the river
West of Rosario Cemetery
Now a little strip mall,
A quiet suburban cul-de-sac.

A page of haiku—
In one, "spitting blood"
Tubercular, the mention
Like Keats' "bright arterial"
Or Shiki writing about peonies.
The solemn, worn out faces
Hands on bent knees.

It is all gone now
Except the trees they planted, and watered—
Or something carried on the wind
As autumn moves to chiller season.
They're not really
Our legitimate ghosts,
Characters engraved on a memorial stone,
Not our ancestors, our dead to feed or placate

Not really our responsibility
And yet . . . a rustle in the last of the leaves
Like a hand passed over a brow
Covering the eyes.

Looking for Miki Hayakawa, 1904-1953

Vase of pink flowers on the window sill,
Painting in a book,
The 1930's, those thick green leaves
Heavy blossoms set
Against a view, beyond the sill
Coit Tower seen from below,
And because it is San Francisco
Tower grey in mist, its deco lines
Speaking of the modern world.
I look the painter up—
Miki Hayakawa—
She's relocated, the text says
To Santa Fe in 1942.
I'm shocked. My own neighborhood here
Sits on the edge
Of what was a Japanese internment camp
By the river, along the Alameda.
Suburban hues today
Still shaded by trees
Those prisoners planted.

It's hard to find out much about her.
The camp was all men, accused of being spies
Imprisoned for crimes like selling rope
In a general store
Or having a stick of dynamite
Used to stun fish
On a boat.

Why did she come here? I can only speculate—
A brother, an ill father, in the camp?
The curator at the museum
Says: oh, of course
She married Preston McCrossen, the painter—
Well-known, if unremembered.
And now her life story shifts.
She lives in an adobe house with bancos,
A Chimayo rug, a blackware pot from San Ildefonso,
Until she dies in early middle-age of cancer.
I can't locate her grave. The marker with Japanese characters
In shady Rosario Cemetery
Is for an internee.
She's gone.

Why do I care?
It's the flowers, in part.
The way the painter
Caught the light
Of a San Francisco room
With fog outside, imagining Pacific
Islands in mist.
It's the forced move inland
Away from a whitewashed room
The smell of the dim sum parlor, the Italian grocery
A park of dogs, bundled children, derelicts
A kind of concentration
On brushstroke color,
The painting "From My Window"
Where Coit Tower
Recedes into mist
As if from the prow of a great seabound ship.

Refugees

You reach the border—
The news isn't good
Your husband is dead, or your father,
Or maybe your mother's brother.
Still, you are alive, if
Exhausted beyond endurance
In the spring air.
It's 1939, or 1999,
You no longer wear
The national costume
Of kerchief and petticoats
But a nice jacket, a cheap knock-off
Of something Italian designed in L.A.;
And you still have your children,
That's important, both of them,
The boy and girl.
Although you fled Tamerlane and Genghis Khan
Hitler and Stalin,
Although you flee this week's strong man
And in the news photo
Your dark eyes look dead
In the back of the truck
Although the news from the interior is not good
Villages burned, mass graves, air strikes
Still, I know from my own experience
That you will cross this border,
Make a living driving a cab
In some great city

Learning to curse in French or English.
Or open a grocery store
With piles of tomatoes and oranges
Even, on the counter, baked delicacies
Dripping pistachios and honey
By the cash register
To sell
A lost taste of home.

Dumpling

First time I tasted
Chinese steamed buns—
We were on a bus in the dark
From Boston to D.C., we wanted to see
The T'ang dynasty horse rear up in porcelain.
Truth is, I wanted you naked
In the nice hotel's bed, that lobby
With the blue enamel ceiling studded with Federalist stars.
Of all the people I've ever loved
You were the most aggravating.
The people from the Yen-Ching Institute
Who had hired the bus
Ran out of money, sold buns and eggrolls en route
Odd, how not until thirty years later
Do I realize they must have been
A recent wave of Harvard's refugees
Intelligentsia who fled on foot.

Many years later in a New Mexico parking lot
I eat a soft wonton out of my daughter's soup
At the Saigon, and suddenly remember
In scallion broth
How many dumplings I've eaten:
Potato piroge from the Russian deli
On 8th and Irving when absolutely no one loved me.

Dumplings wrap things up.
Tidier than life.

Driving out past the Pen on Route 14
The mercantile now lit
With the words "India Palace"
I make my husband stop
Go inside and buy two samosas.
The man behind the counter
With its poster of Krishna
Is far from all of our homes.
The samosas are delicious,
I could have bought tamales too,
Red chile wrapped in corn husks,
Like a doll, the corpse of summer.
Biting down, I make my husband
Eat one too, sip mango juice
Out on the plains, as if in the exact
Center of nowhere.

Artichoke Heart

I cook this prickly thing for you,
Gently manipulate stiff leaves
Beneath cold water tap,
Rinse each hard green petal
Trim the stem, place it in the pot
Steam it. Like Eve
Holding a forbidden fruit
I set it on the table.
Did I stalk your heart?
An artichoke is rare, delicious,
Odd that one can both eat and choke on it.
You dip the pale green
Part of each leaf in butter,
I eat much faster than you do,
I eat more than my share,
"It's like lobster," you say
"I never know
  What part I'm supposed to eat."
"Eat the heart," I say,
Artichoke heart on the stem
Steamy like a naked woman getting out of a bath.
I prune the prickles, slice that heart in half
Hand it to you.
"Saving the best for last?" I tease.
Later, I tell you, you know
You could buy two next time
I'd still cook them for you.
And you say: not until they're on special.

Did I mistake your thrift for love?
Did you really not just want to sit and dip
Those dark green leaves, that pale green heart
That thick stem?
Did you not want to look at me as you licked butter?
Middle-aged, you still have a green heart.
Young, you hitched through Castroville once,
The artichoke capital of the world
But you did not know how to eat an artichoke
Until you ate with me.

Things I Have Eaten

I ate odd things as a child—
Onion grass which grew wild in my father's lawn,
Library paste, my own cuticles.
My daughter confessed
She tried to eat her pre-school
Bit by bit, gouging out
Handfuls of straw and adobe,
Daring her best friend to swallow it.
What I wanted most when I was a child
Was to eat, uninterrupted, an entire jar
Of marinated artichoke hearts.
I grew up in a household of thieves—
Strawberries, artichokes, chocolate chips
Someone would simply reach over
And spear it on a fork.
My Russian grandfather would say—
"Look! A bird!"
Like an idiot, I'd look—
A bird in my mother's breakfast nook?
And wham, half my peach ice cream
Would vanish on his spoon.
Save the best for last, my husband says
With his I.R.A., his savings, his insurance binder.
I save tiny jars of condiments
Pickled eggplant, olives stuffed with almonds,
                              Italian pimentoes

Which I will eat as soon
As I am alone.

Attack of the Killer Husbands

All week long at the gym
I've pedaled further, treadmilled harder
Because of the made for T.V. movies
About the psychopathic killer husbands.
The basic plot is always the same—
The heroine, brunette or blond,
Just wants to be a good
Wife and mother,
But her husband has *changed*—
It's the steroids, or jealousy
Or the fact that he, although handsome, and a dentist,
(Or a cop)
Has already secretly murdered his first wife.
Increasingly isolated
In the nice suburban house
Or palatial redwood cabin
We come to the same scene:
They are eating dinner,
He is enraged about something,
And the look of realization crosses her face—
He'll stop at nothing.

I bike stationary mile after mile
Waiting for the moment
When pushed to the edge
She'll shoot him through the head.
One disconcerting thing is
The killer husband is always in great shape

Works out constantly for the camera
Testosterone pumping, a poor message
For the gym
Linking fitness to murder.
I don't want you to think
I watch these movies
To feel morally superior,
I've had my own troubles
And husbands.
I never even get to see
The end of the movies—
The prison scenes, the defense trial.
They're hours longer than my work-out,
It's just that moment at dinner I like
Where he criticizes the peas, or the steak
And she peers teary-eyed
Over the wine glass rim
And realizes
It's her, or him.

My Life as an Intellectual

The first thing I ever read
That made me see God in narrative
And that I was also in that web
Was Tolkien's
Lord of the Rings.
I must have been eleven, twelve
Sat reading, pillowed in bed
By the light of the rose-colored lamp.
The book became a dangerous thing
When everyone else in the house was asleep.
Finally terrified, I went to wake
My sister, and in a fit of sadism
Sat on her chest to recite
The scary poem at the book's start,
Although she'd squirm and shout
I repeated this night after night
I'd declare about her cries
"In the Land of Mordor where the shadow lies . . ."

Years later, one cold winter, I lived at Yaddo
Writer's colony in Saratoga,
It was so cold, that bad wind out of Canada.
A handful of us walked each evening, after dinner
In bare forest, lit by art deco
Lanterns with panes of swirled pink glass.
In a fit of self-improvement
Brought on by dreadful boredom
I tried to read *The Brothers Karamazov*,

Put it down to cut the deck
Played another hand of Vegas solitaire
Then read uninterrupted four romances by Shakespeare
Of which I retained nothing—not *Pericles* or *Cymbeline*.
I remember the dark trees, though
The dark house, the enormous white
Painter's studio where I was oddly housed to write
And my bedroom with the beautiful lamp
Metal shade set with marbles of glass
Through which an ordinary lightbulb shone
Colors of a fairy land.
So much was wasted on me then—
Love, solitude, even
The lavish regular meals,
I loved that lamp though, casting a meadow
The corners of the room in shadow.

Aristotle

It was a nice party, and snowing
So that arriving guests
Shook themselves off
Before tromping in to the fire.
I was sitting, trapped in a corner,
With three St. John's students
Debating loudly
Aristotle, who, they claimed
Said no one could ever really understand
Anyone else.
I butted in: "what about saying
'I love you madly and will do whatever you want'
Or, 'I left the newspaper on the hall table for you'
Isn't that clear enough?"
No, no, they insisted, no one
Could ever truly hear and understand.
I wanted to say: who lied to you when you
Were little? Who hurt you
So badly with words?
But instead excused myself
Went to the kitchen
Where the host—with whom I had
An utterly complicated
Relationship was doling out someone else's posole.
He offered me a bowl, and I ate it.
Driving home in the snow

My husband went too fast and briefly lost control
Of the car which spun and hit the curb.
And I shouted: hey, slow down
In all this snow
And he did.

Plato's Cave

Sign on the back of a truck ahead of me in traffic:
"It's not dead
If it's not grounded,"
Strange omen the morning after
An aurora borealis broke over our southern house,
Disturbance of sunspots
Unsettling as neon left on in the daytime
Or the notion of virginity.

I've always loved the expression *demivierge*
Only in French can virginity
Be seen as partial
Or a matter of opinion.
I also love the words "dead pawn"
An unclaimed item without a ticket,
Perfectly heavy silver squash blossom necklace
The turquoise hand of Fatíma.

Maze with two headless statues,
Or crenulated sandstone,
Texture of a dream,
Broken bottles shining in the sun
On the rim of Canyon de Chelly.
In last night's dream
I took my students on a field trip
To see a black hole—
Which was, just that—
Black hole beneath Manhattan subway grate.

But when we shone our flashlights on it
Light was swallowed up, could not escape.

What is aniconic?
It means—against images
Like a solitary desert God
Or a Muslim calligrapher.
All my life I've tried
To take the perfect snapshot
Of petunias in a windowbox
Or a drunk on the street
To look through words finally
As if they really were clear water.

The Rat

Our pet hooded rat
Named Mr. Comet
For the star mark on his forehead
Lived in a palatial cage.
We had him trained
To scamper on to our open palms
Grab a peanut, skitter to hide it
In his little house.
He had a rat's hard-scrabble feet,
A feat of engineering tail,
He was so soft, the color of a mink
I loved him, and he liked me, too.

Then one day, someone—
It wasn't me
Left the door ajar—
In came the cat.
By the time we found him
Mr. Comet was clinging terrorized to the bars
So adrenalized he could move
Neither forward not backward.
Suddenly, his little paws
Gave way and he dropped
Like a ripe plum to the sawdust.
He was uninjured, but obviously in shock,
I was sure he would have
A rat sized heart attack.

My daughter wept, turned out the lights
Sat with Mr. Comet in the dark,
Told him he would be all right.

I was surprised, but the child's knowledge
Proved correct,
By the next morning
He scampered as ever
Whiskers a-quiver
Up one of my shoulders
And down the next.
He seems happy, to this day;
Still, I can't help but wonder
If his rat soul awoke to the existence of danger
He who had been raised
Without reference to predator or prey,
Petted, hand fed,
Suddenly seeing his natural enemy.
And the cat?
She seemed different at first
Obviously top of the food chain
Designed for one thing.
But soon that faded too,
She purred in my lap,
I was the only creature here
Who wasn't natural in the habitat
Who kept wanting
To make meaning of what had happened
To all of us
To cat, rat, child, and me—
To tell the story.

Keys

Today I copied the house keys
For numerous people who will lose them

A key cannot replicate by sexual reproduction
Like a pink lily, or a woman

It is passive, must be cut and trimmed
By the locksmith, who invariably flirts with me

When I was young, keys made me sad,
Copied keys to temporary apartments

But now approaching fifty
I know I am not alone

Everyone has a key to someplace long gone
Or one whose use is forgotten

I am not the only one hoarding a dead man's key
To a truck sold off years ago

Now I no longer expect, as I did as a child
To find a key lying on the sidewalk before me

Tiny key to a jewelry box lined with mirrors
Green rusted key to the perfect locked garden.

Hatched

Suddenly, because it rains
Ten thousand moth eggs hatch in our house

Moths shade the porch light
Like a living Japanese paper lantern

Hummingbird moths sip nameless purple flowers
Some people call them sphinx moths

They live on white pyracantha blossoms
Or nap in the crevices of our laundry

Shake the negligee—moths
Shake the boxer shorts—more of the same

The newspaper says we are not alone
The entire town is full of moths

Golden stars on the blue enamel sky
At the Masonic Temple unfold their wings

Butterflies too, everywhere,
Swallowtail, orange wing . . .

We have taken
To complaining about butterflies as well

One thing I know
Watching my twelve year old daughter

Stare moodily at the paste-on stars
On the ceiling of her room

Nothing will ever
Go back to its cocoon.

Fairy Tale

You brought bread but neglected the brick of salt
Did you expect me then to live in happiness?
All night long the pine trees make a dark sound
As if they did not fear the woodcutter.
I bleached the floor boards with white sea sand
Breadcrumbs flew from your beard like birds.
Don't read that fairy tale aloud tonight
In which the brothers turn into ravens,
The sister must journey to the glass mountain
Use the bone in her little finger as a key.
What is this exclamation point! And in the middle of a line—
It tells me I am right to doubt that you love me.

Nude with a Gas Mask

After September 11, my friends began shopping
For gas masks, toilet paper, Cipro.
When I was a child, my mother used to take me to
                             the Cloisters
By Spuyten Duyvil, past Yonkers, across from the Palisades.
We both loved the treasury the best
Monkey cup enameled with dozens of tiny
Monkeys among vines. I like St. Anthony's Cross
With a compartment for an allopathic herbal dose
Against ergot madness.
That is when I first became afraid
Of medieval rye madness that makes one hallucinate
Despite the fact
It is not found in New Jersey
In this century. But I still
Won't drink from an open can of coca cola
In case it has LSD in it.
After September 11 my friends began planning
How to evacuate Manhattan in case of disaster.
If the bridges were sealed
There was no way out.
They began shopping for life jackets and flotation devices
So they could swim the East River
Land in a terrifying no-man's land
Of drug dealers and gangsters on the other side.
At the Cloisters my mother explained to me
How the stone effigies of knights on tombs

Had the legs crossed if he'd been in the crusades.
And the unicorn, did I mention that white beast
Trapped not by lances but a pure virgin
And forced into a paradise of flowers?

The Sociology of Unforeseen Consequences

You in that cap—we could be anywhere
Bessarabia, 1905—speaking Yiddish
Time travel to a place
That produces only rugs and massacres
Like Canyon de Chelly,
A bad night in Chinle, Arizona . . .

The capitals of the cloister's columns
Crawling with goblin faces and semi-domesticated monsters—
This was the old world
Before St. Joseph's eyes were painted open.
The mariachi horn player was Jewish and from Chicago,
Off-season, the garlic farmer worked as a bill clerk
For the state legislature.
The other bill clerks were santeros,
In the down time
One painted St. Joseph's eyes.
A santero should be a holy person.
I felt awkward, as a Jew, in a museum full of madonnas
                                        and crucifixes
But not here, in the north, so far
From the centers of power
Many months from the Inquisition in Mexico City.
Here, where straw is inlaid
Instead of gold,
Where so many of us
Take care of things
Not originally ours
But which fell to our care.

Looking at Paintings. Washington, D.C.

Ladies in kimonos lounge
On a balcony
Against the smoke of factories
At Battersea—
Whistler, 1864

Outside the gallery
Federal buildings look imperial
Arches dedicated
To forgotten secretaries of agriculture,
Headlines of war.

European model in Japanese dress
Leafing through woodblock prints
Not just the facade of pattern
But gunboat diplomacy
Butterfly—Hiroshima
Blue of indigo fabric
Burned on flesh.

Then, Vuillard
Luminous rooms—bride, corset
A table set for lunch—
Betrayal—
What the painter really wants from the model.
This century is not going to work out well for all of us.
Reds, yellow—a china plate
Green of landscape.

Rain in the actual city
Grey sky, magnolias
Opening from tinted buds.
War, air bombardment, rain, the colors
Of an advertisement blur
On a passing bus . . . .

Homage to Mary Colter

I thought it was real . . .
Hopi House on the canyon's rim
As real, no, more real
Than Hopi itself
When I was a child
When we took the Superchief in the snow
When I first caught a glimpse
Of what I would desire—
Ladder leading to an opening
In roof, or wall,
The imagined West.

Sitting in the French pastry shop
At La Fonda Hotel
On east San Francisco Street
I've sat and drunk excellent coffee
Through snowstorms, through grief.
Pastries, strawberry and chocolate, in the glass case
Shining brass pans, rustic chandeliers—
So many interiors
Where I felt at peace
Were designed by the same architect.

Do you remember
That time, your first
Driving to the rim
As dusk fell out of Flagstaff
Songs on the AM radio

Seemed to choreograph
Our mood, barely enough daylight
Left to get there in time for a glimpse.
And at the first lookout
There it was—Canyon el Grande
That ocean made of color and shape.
The look on your face.

I saw it when I wasn't even
Twelve, that place
With eagle dancers in the light snow
Outside the false pueblo.
Now older, I know I can't answer
What is authentic—
Like fancy dancers on the pow wow circuit.
But then, I just believed it was true
Those dancers in their great
Black and white wings
Heel toe, heel toe.

La Posada. Winslow, Arizona

. . . that first moment
Of stepping on the train
Stepping up,
It's that moment
I love the most
That requires
A long skirt, the right hat—
An attitude of pure departure . . .

Sitting on the train
Looking out the darkened window to the scene
That's when I realized
My God, this was that dream
Recurring, riding high
On rails that flash by
Closed unblinking towns
Until the conductor calls the name
Of disembarkment—
My whole life I dreamed I was asleep
As if sleep were a vehicle
From literal place to place.

Mary Colter built this hotel.
Tonight in the cold
We walk towards it from the train
Leaving one lit place and entering another.
Narrative transformed to architecture,
This place does not begin with block and tile

But a story she must tell herself
Though why stays as a mystery.
Her imaginary family
Comes from Spain, prospers, adds a wing
(See—here is the falsified exterior wall)
Grows rich in cattle, ballrooms, guests
Now it is we who've come to call
As if this tale were real.

Girl child of the mid-Victorian
Who for some reason
Collects the drawings of the Sioux
Crayon colored hunters on horseback.
An outbreak of smallpox,
Her mother tries to burn them
Destroy a hypothetical contagion.
The child fights back
To preserve these artifacts, her first feeling.
As a woman she will become
An excavator of imagination
A woman alone, without child or husband
Wearing numerous necklaces at once,
Rings on many fingers,
Inlaid stones shaped like footprints
Trekking across turquoise or obsidian,
And another one—
Ring of a coral hand
Wearing itself a tiny blue ring . . .
Mementos of a repeatable creation.
At breakfast
A man I have just met tells me

How he hit a deer
In his old truck.
He has been waiting for this for years.
Later, he argues with me about fate.
Having come this far in middle-age
I have heard enough
Of what men say to women—
Beyond seduction, it's the sound
Of their own story they love
The way when young
They might have loved
The image of a woman,
Still, it's certain that alone in this big bed
With its mission headboard
Set in the park of winter trees
Where the trains wake every sleeper
You are the one I love—
That is what I called to say.

In the Valentine Diner
Also with its art deco lines
Angela, daughter of the former owner Irene
With her big dark eyes, serves green chile.
The blind Navajo named Henry
Stirs his coffee loudly
Asks our names, then tells a story:
There were once three girls—
Good riders, very good
Horseback riders
They were riding
Away from the Spanish cavalry.

You've heard of them? Conquistadors.
The girls ran in different directions
Oh, they would rather have stayed together
But for the soldiers
One goes north, one east, one west—
The Salt Clan—that's how it scattered.
Then he says to us:
"I can't see what people look like.
If I met you again
I wouldn't know who you were . . ."
Getting on the train.

In the lobby of the grand hotel
Festival of the Trees
Dozens of pines lit up
With fairy lights, glass globes, glitter of angel wings
Little girl gasps first
Then in the center of the great tiled floor
Starts spinning
Trying to bring outside
What is inside
Like anyone who can see
Dizzy with the joy of shining tree.

Hundreds and Thousands:
Journal of Emily Carr

I walked to the Empress Hotel
Straight into the conservatory
Most of the guests were still in bed
The conservatory was empty of humans—
Just the flowers, and they were at worship
And let me join them:
Cyclamen, pink, red
Rose, little pink begonia
Calla lilies, feathery palms
And all the while I sat quite quiet.

Don't cultivate parsons out of their pulpits
They are quite disappointing.
The mountain is finished
And the tree with the moving background.
The roof seems low and heavy.
My new sketches thrill me.
My landscapes look somehow lacking and dark.
How completely alone I've had to face the world.

It makes you feel so old
When they say: "What a lot of work"
People said "explain the pictures"
Perhaps I do not know
Any more than they.
How tired one can get and not die!

Rain drops hit the roof
The green of the thin flat leaves is clear
Water drips from leaf to leaf.
I love the earth, and am afraid
Of the infinity of the sky.
A blue sky recedes wave upon wave
The trees are wave upon wave of quiet grey.
What does it matter anyway?
Big things bump into you, bruising
Little things chafe and nag
Being old is not bad if you keep away from mirrors.
Everything holds its breath except spring.

Brautigan

The afternoon we heard Richard Brautigan had shot himself
Phil Whalen insisted we go to the bar
At the La Fonda Hotel
Sit in the darkened room out of the desert light
Drink margaritas, the slightly bitter ones
They make there, heavy on the lime, light on the salt.
God, that was such a long time ago—
The Plaza was so different then,
You could buy a needle and thread at Woolworth's,
The center of town had a quiet feel,
Dark leaves blowing in autumn,
Cottonwood fuzz in spring,
Summer brought tourists
Like a flock of birds
That would eventually depart
To someplace else.
I guess you could say
I was still wandering then,
Perhaps I am even today
When I pick ripe apricots from the tree
You watered but never saw bear fruit.
Today I watched it rain
Lay on the couch
Read a book by Brautigan's daughter
Remembered, like suddenly smelling the sea
Inland, taste of those margaritas
In the darkened bar
A second hand taste of grief.

You Ate Phil Whalen's Noodles
FOR M.B.

You give a full report of the funeral
Who was missing, who was there
About the procession of offerings—
Peanut brittle, an orchid, a big bowl of Chinese noodles.
It's curious, we note
How after every death
The divvying up begins
The "who owns Phil"
Memory, reputation, manuscripts.
Even I can't help but mention
The many times I took him to the dentist,
Paid for the internist,
How frequently Robert
Cooked him blini with caviar.
Now you tell me
That after the ceremony
At Kathie and Norman's on Muir Beach
You all actually ate
The Chinese food offering, those delicious
Noodles for supper.
I'm so jealous I can barely speak
Or tell you what I meant to
In the face of loss
How glad I am
To have thought so well of you
For almost twenty years.

Figa

I must have been drunk
That cold night at the party
When the famous nut brown lady poet
Untied my blue velvet sash
I must have been drunk
Up in that north country
My dress didn't fall off
The sash came off in her hand
She was a small woman
With a fringe of bangs
Like a Scandinavian squirrel
A mouse hoarding nuts and seeds

I must have been drunk
When turning I pulled the pink bow
That tied her blouse to her neck
It opened, and revealed
A charm shaped like a black fist
Making an obscene gesture
I must have been shocked
To see the bird being flipped
In miniature around her spinster's neck.
"Elizabeth Bishop gave me this," she said
"From Brazil,"
As if I'd opened
A nest of Russian dolls—
Inside one poet
Was an even better poet.

I must have been drunk
I left that party with two boys
Went back to the cabin of one
The fair one, not the dark
Drank so much whiskey
We began to see the molecules in the air
Tripping our brains out.
Neither of them touched me
I must have been drunk
To have slept on the floor like that
She'd have kissed me—I'm quite sure of that.
She's been dead a long time now.
I must have been drunk.

Choreographer

When I was sixteen I danced choreographed
To Mahler's Fifth symphony, the fourth movement
Adagietto—that summer at sleep-away camp
Where sweaty at the barre with girls who cared
And could do much more than me
We stretched in reflection.
The ballet master hit me on the knee—
"Think here, think with your knee"
He said in that voice
Which evinced worship in some
Obedience in all.
I couldn't place him then, mysterious, and cool
Toward our bodies, it was only as an adult I realized
He was a contemporary of Cage's, Cunningham's,
Gay, a modernist, hooked on D.T. Suzuki
New York style Zen.
After class, we'd leap into the pool
Hold one pose or another
Briefly underwater
And on the night of the performance
Float to what seemed
The world's loveliest music
Competing with cicadas and crickets.
Once in the evening we sat at his feet
And he talked, about exactly what I cannot reconstruct
Impermanence? Or—concentration?
And looking up, I saw his head glow

With an aura, a saint's halo
And didn't even realize then
He was the first of many masters
I didn't choose to follow.

Translating Catullus

At fifteen or sixteen I could translate lines
Of raw sex and rawer love
Straight out of the Latin
Like: that guy over there
Looks like a god
Just because he gets to sit next to you . . .

I went to girls' school where I wore
Plaid uniform skirt illegally rolled
Short above the thigh, and pink cumberbund
Also illegal, neatly tied
Around my fabric fat waist.

Catullus was not my first
Boyfriend, I'd already lost
That hindrance not worth clinging to
A cumbersome virginity.
I could also decline
Verbs in three languages.

Still, even I was shocked
Reading ahead, the lyric unassigned
Where the poet comes across a couple making love
Then did something I could barely visualize.

Hell, this was New Jersey, 1969
Everything was about to change

And I was itching
To riot in the street, throw a brick
Through a plate glass window . . .

Instead, I sat in my white man-tailored
Shirt and grey blazer
Following the track of dactyls, elegaics
Knew when the poet said "passer"—sparrow
He meant something more personal.

He spoke to me—Catullus—
My second boyfriend.
The class set a modern dance to him
Floated with chiffon scarves
Beneath maple and elm
Coached someone's little brother
To stand still and drop a white flower
At the end to these words:
"Cut down by the plow."

Truly, I don't know
Any more now
Than I did then
Of hate and love
Of desire that consumes
And will consume
Whatever you may feed it.

War

Pumpkins sit on the porch,
Bound sheaves of corn stalk,
Warty gourds in a centerpiece
On the polished table
And, back-lit by late autumn light
She stands with a platter
In both hands, roasted meat
Resting on the rose and leaf pattern.
She faces them—the sullen
Fourteen year old daughter with a scowl
The stoned, absented sixteen year old boy
Her husband, her brother—known as Uncle Charlie the
                                        fucking
                                        warmonger
Watch your mouth!
But it's true . . . baby killer
While you still live in my house, young lady . . .
And her sister-in-law, Charlie's wife, the three tow-headed
                                        children.
They'll barely bless the food and it begins
The war about the war
The accusations—"napalm," "coward"
And the girl bolts first from the table
In tears, up to her room
To turn the music up high
And smoke the butt end of a cigarette.
Then the aunt snaps at the uncle—
"Goddamit, Charlie

Can't we eat together just once in peace,
Your sister cooked for hours . . ."
A sigh, a smile between the women.
He pounds on the table with his fist,
"What makes this country great"
And "sacrifice."
Turning to the boy who chews
Potatoes, peas, stuffing, bread
Who can eat through anything
Says: "Son, you'll serve if called,"
"Nope, I'm going to Canada,"
"You're what!" the boy's father shouts
He swore he'd remain neutral, quiet
The master of his tongue and house
"No son of mine . . ."
He's not thinking coward . . . instead
But who will run the business?
You're smart. Give me grandchildren.
The girl probably won't.
His wife is still standing
This time with pie
Her husband looks at her
She's white knuckled around the pink scalloped plate.
Charlie's wife leaps up, herding kids
"I'm sorry, no dessert. We're going home."
They're gone. Leaves blow in the street
Its dusk along the east coast
The son eats, a slice of moist cake.
The daughter curses in her room
Plots her escape
No Canada for her, she wants New York.
The husband looks at his wife

He loved her once.
That was a different war. He breathes.
He loves her still.
"Next time," he says "I'll take you out to eat."
"But family," she says, "the holidays . . . I have to cook . . ."
"I can't stand it anymore. I'll take you out alone.
 Fuck them all. We'll eat Italian, something."
She smiles, and as if released
The cup slips from her hand
One of the four gold rimmed ones left
From her maternal grandmother
The one that matches
The lovely platters . . .
It slips. It shatters.

Good Girls

When I grew up,
There were bad girls in white lipstick,
Good girls in shirtwaists.
When I grew up
The truth is: all girls were bad
Our bodies like concealed weapons
Ready to fire.
I'd stare at myself
In the greenish wavy mirror over the sink
In the Port Authority Bus Station ladies' room,
I was alert as if for combat,
I never hung my bag on the hook
On the inside door
I never sat directly on the toilet seat
I never touched the handle of the toilet
Instead, I had mastered
The art of flushing a toilet with my foot
Something I can still do to this day.
As a result, I was never cut, raped, or mugged
My naked body
Was never dumped down an elevator shaft—
A possibility which threatened my imagination.
When I was 14
Only sailors had tattoos
We did not pierce our tongues
Heroin addicts sat on panels at our school
Told us not to smoke pot or we would go mad.

I would have enjoyed
Writing all over my body,
Face and torso, arms and legs
But all I really had to say
Could have fit on the bridge of my nose:
Good-bye. I'm gone.

Florida: The Water Bird

Florida is
New Jersey's
Lost paradise
Garden with an alligator.
Something with teeth—
Eve's pearly whites
Punctured apple flesh,
Look what we have—
Strip mall, pesticide, a rude
Customer undertipping the waitress.
Florida is
Where New Jersey goes
Not after death, but before—
Runaways, failed dope dealers,
Old Ukrainian Jews
Who want to die by the sea
But inexplicably live on.
Art deco moon,
Arabian palm.

I have to say
It bothered me
The large hand painted sign
By the Everglades
Proclaiming: Robert is here.
My first husband Robert
Has been dead for five years
But I stop anyway

Just in case I've been mistaken.
But I don't find him among papayas, coconuts
Carved in crabbed, ugly, shrunken heads
Or a good price on conch shells
Or something green and shriveled
By the cash register
Claiming to be chocolate pudding fruit
You can eat with a spoon when ripe.

He wasn't there, although of course
In life he might have been,
A greengrocer who liked the subtropics
Who as a kid ran from Jersey to Fort Lauderdale
Lived in a tent pitched
In an otherwise furnitureless apartment
With a half dozen others.
His "job" was to pick the girls up
At the strip joint
Walk them home
Across the dangerous parking lot.
Then he ran further, to Key West
Lived on the beach with sleeping bag and lobster fork,
There, at the absolute
Boundary between pastel and continent
Lived like a pelican
On cast off sport fish,
Turned seventeen,
Wondered what would happen next.

The water hyacinth
Also is not native here
Though beautiful, will strangle,

Clog the propeller, delay the boat's
Departure through alleyed estuary.
There's little difference here
From fresh to salt,
Sky or earth, a brackish
Puddle that gives birth.
Like a lotus from muddy water—
Roots in slime,
Pure white blossom,
In the sullied stream, white egret
On legs' delicate stalk
This image of perfection,
This image of regret.

Anxiety

How often I've longed
For a really long book to read
To relieve my suffering—
Waiting in the dentist's office, or
My heart broken . . .
Something like *The Makioka Sisters*
Written during war, or *The Tale of Genji*
Or *Magic Mountain* or even
Something fat and trashy
For a day at the beach.

I used to sit on the sand
Of the perfectly wide and clear
Beach outside my grandmother's
Art Deco building.
It wasn't until forty years later
Again on Miami Beach
Watching the tankers and freighters
Float as if weightless in the broad shipping channel
That I saw that turquoise water
All the way to Cuba
All the way to Tierra del Fuego
Like an Otis Redding song
Like a David Hockney swimming pool
Like something you don't even
Have to tire yourself out
Comparing to something.
Then I realized

Well, that was beauty
That was what I'd seen in the dream
That was what gave me the taste
For the edge
Of continents
Among other things.

The Bridge of Discontinuity

Iconographic blue, blurred
Nexus of sky and sea

Analogous to the causeway
Old bridge abruptly missing in mid-arch

Crossing this sheer space
How fate is like the mind

One thing leads to another
Overheard snatches of conversation

Interrupted narrative
How the past changes by the insertion of the present

Like the arrival of a pelican
Thinking you have fish at the end of the pier

Even the great reptile by the dark ditch
Has a cache of eggs that will or will not hatch

Who can say—what I wanted has come to pass
You always tell me I worry too much

We could have walked for miles on the sandbar
Ankle deep in turquoise water

This is the line where God's name should appear
Instead a large umbrella, drunkenly tipped by the breeze

Starts to blow seaward in the prevailing
Wind that lifts beyond the jetty's rail

Red umbrella, dark pink sail . . .

Spiral Hill—White Sand and Peat Blocks
Graphite and Brown Ink on Paper. Robert
Smithson, 1971

Ziggurat of Babylon, Tower of Babel
Terraced pyramid in the left-hand corner,
Then a double line which divides the paper
Almost equally in half
Like a horizon in which there is slightly more land than sky.

When I was a child, I looked everywhere for burial mounds,
I knew about barrows built over kings
Whole Viking ships covered by a wave of earth.
This was in New Jersey in the Fifties—
A place flat as Holland and settled by the Dutch
Where sea-level was only three steps down off the
                                        boardwalk.
I hoped that every little rise or hill
Covered in grass contained a warrior, hands clasped.
Late at night I'd read
About Egyptian pyramids and Aztec tombs,
What the Mayans threw down a well
Or the great mounds of Ohio.

In the sky there is also a spiral uncoiling
Shaped like a snail uncurling
Across the right-hand quadrant of the page.
Some people say there is a difference between a labyrinth
                                        and a maze
That a labyrinth has false turns

While a maze leads straight to the center.
I have read many books with "maze" and "labyrinth"
                                                in the title
But have been unable to confirm this.

Last night I dreamed you left me
That recurring dream
Whose meaning must be something else.
I make you swear you'll never leave
In the kitchen nonetheless.
How can I be sure
We are speaking the same language
As I brew coffee
This day's syntax and schematic?

To Begin Outside the Bar

To begin outside the bar
In the Best Western in Grants, New Mexico
And try and tell the truth about my life
I want to finally focus
On something large, like the land mass
Of a continent, or the old
Black lava flow of El Malpais
Which shadows the by-passed two-lane.
My problem is
I have been talking about the same things
For a long time, namely—myself
Also the beauty that takes one unawares:
A swollen window frame
Painted turquoise,
Clay pot shaped like a woman
Planted with geraniums.
Only in this landscape
There is something
That compels people to keep walking
Sometimes almost aimlessly
On the shoulder of the highway
As if their car had broken down
Or they were drunk, or broke
Walking by stones and sagebrush
As if the Greyhound hadn't come
Or they lacked change for a phone call
As if we were walking home.

Zero: Canyon de Chelly

We hiked down
Glorious red rock, hogan, fields, penned sheep
Through the bosque, and crossed the river
On a small flat bridge that hadn't been there
When I was young.
White House was newly fenced as well
But just as beautiful, cliff ruin.
I sat in the sun and stared
At a world made visible.
My hair was pulled up in a ponytail beneath my cap
I sat there long enough
To get a first degree burn that peeled for days
I'd forgotten
Myself, I was so struck
By the unstartling thought
"I'm just the same as I ever was."
It seemed to take a second to understand it
Or the half hour it took to burn my neck
Or the forty-six years it took
To get me to that particular rock
Or six centuries to ruin White House
Or a million years to grind that canyon down
Or a few hours to hike back up
Or a year to write this poem
Or a quarter of an hour before bed
Or twenty years since I was first there
That other time, which was also the first time
I suddenly understood everything.

Petrified Forest: Lot's Wife

What was once wood,
Now gem-like stone, mineralized.
Tall trees of the Triassic—
Woodworthia, Schilderia,
Washed into silt, mud, volcanic ash.
Silicon deposits
Crystalize into quartz,
Log of amethyst.
You say, oddly sad.
Well, rock will never
Become wood
No matter how long
Time passes.
As a chid, I simply thought
Each tree had sucked the mineral colors in
Jasper red, pale orange, lavender
Drawn up by the roots with water.
Now older, I mistrust
Memory as any kind of fact;
Lot's wife too
Turned suddenly crystal
From the shock of looking back.

The Weaver's Line

"My name is Manuelito Lovato"

That's what it says on the tag
Of the small woven rug
I bought in Los Ojos,
A place that implies water.

"I was born in Coyote, New Mexico"

Not far from Tierra Amarilla
Passing the billboard that says in Spanish
"Land or Death", and knowing it's not that easy
Most of us have neither.

"Seventeen years later I married"

The dark blue rug with a red zigzag
Shaped like a mountain or an electrocardiogram
Or a blue woolen sky
Split by lightning

"The weaver is dead"

That is what the cashier said
When I took the rug to the counter
Prepared to pay
My hard earned hundred dollars

"She got the cancer and died"

No more small blue rugs from this loom
Blue of chicory and Abiquiu dam under rain
Red of a heart line
Or something remembered

"I was born in 1934"

She started weaving at the age of forty-nine
Her eleven year old grandson taught her
But what taught her to weave like that
That bold red thread on blue wool?

Counting the Omer

Old Laguna—
cloud stepped steeple, white church
snow on Mount Taylor

Conquistador's
signature on sandstone
clear in the rain

Zuni hornos
steaming in the rain, baking
bread, Easter feast day

Making love—
sound of one train
after another

whistle of the train
potsherd silence
. . . .

road to the pueblo
closed for Easter, red bud
by the river

crow hopping
lifted
my dark mood

after you showed me
the comet—we didn't
quarrel at all

panic attack—
breathing into paper bag—
evening star

by mistake, black cat
locked in the closet, we're both
faintly embarrassed

mole on my back
worries me—then just
falls off

funny, the smokers
enjoy it most—
blossoming plum

she shows me
what she painted in anger—
sweet pink and yellow

Chinese mountain—
many shades of
monochrome . . .

after a death
pasting ripped black paper
into a blank book . . .

plastic roses
in a planter . . .
this drought

your dead grandmother's
worn ten dollar bill buys
our margaritas

Zen priest
eats half
my brownie

"Jack Frost," old man says
"didn't get my cherry tree
this year . . ."

pregnant woman—
her crescent moon
smile

"ant"—
the tiny girl
bends down

his field burning
all night long, the poet
digs a firebreak

fingernail left
in corrugated
Mimbres potsherd

mortician's girlfriend
says he is a very
patient man

old blue spruce
sheds too many needles—
dwarf peach blossoms

home sick
my young daughter
seems younger

overheard—"No one
is just good, or evil."
"Well, duh."

what do they dream
about at night—
people rushing past

dog barking—
in the next room
her thin cough

all this weather
in from the west—
still no rain

hauling water
I track needles
from the dead spruce

after listening
to gossip of bad husbands
I hug you hard

I turn away
from the headlines—back
to my own worries

"I feel
like an undertaker"—
tree man in drought

grey in my hair—
more pronounced
this spring?

news clip of war—
we pedal on
at the gym

I drive my friend's
children—she visits
her friend with cancer

gardening gloves
on worn sandals—
purple iris

view from the swing
and then
view of my feet

no purple
in pastel box to capture
penstemons

ten days
influenza—
lilacs full bloom

red finches mate—
students flirt
on the patio

songs you taped—
how they bring back
your presence

dancing to "Layla"
I'm almost fifty
singing along still

if you weren't dead
we'd just stay up all night
talking

Venus
the dead spruce
his warm hand

counting the rings—
this tree was as old
as I am

cold spring
withered forsythia
flowers late

candle
in the mirror
sound of rain

Black Ollas

Because you have crossed the border back into your
                                            own country
The blimp which hangs like a devil's hawkeye
Across the Arizona-Sonora border
Casts no shadow in your dreams
Although you may dream of an enclosed courtyard
Of boat-tailed grackles
And a neglected pool
Of the dining room in which only one wall is painted blue
A creamy blue like the hem of the Virgin
And all the other walls are yellow
Although you might remember the twin towers of
                                        the church
Painted a mustard yellow with circles of Chinese red
Which seem to bleed
And how you bought two black ollas
Polished as if by a deranged ocean
To the sheen of mica
Marked with the labyrinths
Of a lost city of mud brick
And although the old man who sold pots
Told you: I am very tired
I am so very tired
And although along the church's walls
Were homemade scenes of papier-mache
Including Adam and Eve in a grotto
And although we made love in a motel room
And I woke to the smell of blood

Although I dreamed about cacao
Jaguarless night far to the south
Or shells from the sea of Cortez
Or a necklace of turquoise
Or sacrifice
Or bones hung from the ceiling
Or roadway shrines with their grills
As if to keep
All saints from escaping
The little houses prepared for them
Now because I have crossed
Back into the north
From country that shows no division in the first place
I might dream of potholes
But not for long
In the white noise, in the laundered dream
Of these united states . . .

Paquimé

who departed suddenly in night and fire
leaving behind penned macaws
a giant mound in the shape of a bird
the egg that hatches death . . .

Between Christmas and New Year's
We went walking
With the families of Chihuahua
Among the ruins of the plain
Kids running, ladies in high heels and blue jeans
Walking over ancestors
Who weren't exactly ours
But neither were they bones we could ignore.
A civic mound, the deep grave of a king.
A copper key cast by lost wax process,
Keyhole shaped doors,
The shape of a man hung upsidedown
"For defense" the sign says in English
But in the museum
There is the exact magical shape for an alabaster altar,
A portal into somewhere else . . .
I'd never seen
A heap of metates in perfect condition
Never used, not one grain of corn
Ground on this stone
Manufactured by a guild of this great town
And left unsold.
Instead we see

What time will grind,
The ruined city
Imitating, as if on purpose,
The shape of the ring of mountains
Walking around them.

Call it war . . .
The ball ring where the loser must die
Or is it the winner?
A city rich in feathers and shells
Rich in curved pottery and gods . . .
Which they did not leave volitionally
Unprepared for the attack
Marauders, or like the Achaeans
Those who wait
Besiege
The wealth of the high house town
And citizens run, leaving
Turkeys in their pens
Fledgling macaws
Agave hearts half baked
In the district of ovens
Where they cooked towards tequila.
The weaver drops the spindle now . . .
And turns, aghast

Abraham leaves Sodom and Gomorrah
Lot's nameless wife must turn and look
You take my photograph
Posed against a beautifully crafted
Mud wall, the still intact brick.

Measuring The Moon

You say—it's an optical illusion
How enormous
The white face of the moon
Appears due east in the late afternoon
Right over Hatch, New Mexico

Illusion, in that, you explain
If you frame the moon
With two fingers
The width remains the same
Even when the moon rides high in the evening sky.
That gesture—thumb parted from first finger—
Which in the United States
Means "just a little bit"
But in Mexico means "please—
Give me a moment."

A Fever

Xipe Totec—god of spring
death mask with a gaping mouth
demands blood
a human sacrifice

haven't you felt that way yourself
smelling the fruit tree blossoms
before the green leaves,
looking down the highway
homesick for someplace
you have never been . . .

Cartography of Memory

Dead reckoning in middle age
Trying to locate where I am going
Which has somehow blurred in the open field
Scrub of prickly pear, stunted pinon, ant hills.
The compass and the map—like directions on the page
Impair my ability to remember
It is the bottle tree which provides location
A cholla cactus skeleton hung
With blue glass bottles.

The bottle tree comes from the Congo
Grants wishes, protects houses
Captures spirits (those voices moaning in the wind)
Because the tricksy souls go in
The narrow neck and can't get out again
A bottle tree
Might also be a family
With many problems
It also marks the turn-off—left or right.
In a way, it is the opposite of a *descanso*
Wayside crosses adorned with ribbons, photographs,
ornaments
That marks the accident, the one-way aimed at death.
Trying to locate myself in time
I'm forced to locate myself in space
A leftover from childhood
Where the spatial defines experience
When time is endless.

The map of my eighteenth summer
Has Foster Street at its center
The hot untidy flat
Sublet from graduate students.
Stepping out—down three
Concrete steps and on to the sidewalk
Across, a turn, on the way to the bus stop
I saw the embryo
Of some small creature
A mouse, a squirrel?
Lying by the curb,
Something dislodged from a nest by the rain.
All I can say is—it disturbed me,
Away from home, living with a boy.
I stepped over it day after day
Until ants carried what was left away.
I spent that summer riffling
Through other peoples' things—
A box of records yielded
Mimi and Richard Farina singing
"Children of Darkness."
And the public library coughed up
A half dozen skinny volumes by Anne Sexton
Which I misguidedly read
To cheer myself up.
I also, in the lab, measured a coleus's breath,
That leafy plant called Jacob's Coat
Inhaled and exhaled along a straw
Filled with colored liquid
Like a small patient on life support.
If Foster Street, and the mattress on the floor
We shared was the center

Then at the right hand—east—lay
The whole shore of the Atlantic
Rocky coast of boulders
Covered in barnacles and mussels
Long trailing weeds I also drew, measured.
I cared about botany then
And if you loved me
But by winter
I would change my major.

At the start of the story, someone leaves home
At the start, everyone leaves
Headed towards a different destination.
Fitzgerald taught me how to take the poem down
Line by line.
In his shabby office I sat and translated.
I broke the meter where
The dancers stumbled
But still I did not win the contest
Translating the original.
Some afternoons Fitz was grey, ashen
An ulcer, or worse
Sent him to lie down on his cot
Until my knock roused him
And he'd sit up, rumpled, in his suit.
Now, he is long dead
But I can read his Odyssey aloud
With my thirteen year old,
Fitz translates Calypso as
"The nymph with the pretty braids."
It all reads as fresh
As if we'd dropped in at a party

Heard this story.
My daughter
Reads smoothly, sometimes
Hesitating to pronounce a name.
Her magenta dyed hair
Pulled back in a ponytail.
She wears her tie-dyed p.j.'s.
After Fitzgerald died
I dreamed of him on his cot
In a dense wood
Sitting up, uncrumpling his tie
In a grove of trees.

Each person's day is a private map.
The souvenir contains the landscape,
The view we have just passed through—
Red rock, stone tunnels, river on our left
(We're heading south out of the Pueblo)
So I'll stop
And buy a beautiful egg shaped pot
From an old man, whose wife painted it
With grandmother spider centered in her web
Eight legs distributed on strands,
A ring of medicine flowers, polychrome
And the rest of the egg painted in geometric black
Tiny squares divided by half
Pattern crissing and crossing, optical illusion
That indicates the clouds for rain.
No wonder I want this spider
Signifying discipline as much as center
Place of emergence
As if wherever you stood
Were home.

Garment Industry

Here, where no one knows the date of Easter
New Jersey among Armenians, Greeks, Russians, Jews,
Constantine's Empire split
Along the division of rivers
History became directional—east, and west
Which ends ambiguously on the shore of a new world
Which clings to its notion that there is no past.
America has three borders:
    Canada
    Mexico
    salt water
America has three borders
    sleep
    wheat
    the dead

I was raised among coats
Racks and racks
I had a spring coat, that oxymoron
A new one every year
Where factories obscured the sky
Above vegetable gardens.
We paid cash, and got what?
A notion of beauty?
If the button could speak
It would tell of the needle in its eye.
The union cutters

Trace the parts in sticky chalk
Like the outline of a corpse in the street.
If the button could speak
It would tell of holes, attachments,
A story of ice skating, braids, braided bread
Now insert
Hitler or Stalin
For the same ending.

In Siberia
The cloud has a cooking pot
The cloud has a family
That lives together in a tent of mist
The north star is a stake to tether horses
Spirit of smallpox
Cannibalizes flesh
This world is animate
Lamps that walk about at night
Antlers that shift on graves
Knife of bone.

Raised among coats
Lovely yellow and pink
Like Joseph with his coat of many colors
I also left home
Sold downstream
In the palace of strangers
Became an interpreter of dreams.
Rag—a scrap of cloth
    to taunt
    to scold

Hope—how can you speak of it,
What is hope but heart panic delayed?
This coat will warm you in the parade
Easter, Thanksgiving, St. Pat's, Puerto Rican
                                        Independence Day.
Were we by hope betrayed?
Did we exchange our freedom for a cage?
Was this prison of our own making?
The city hums with commerce
We traded day for neon light
Trim and pile arrayed,
The smell of home for a new last name
In the rag trade.

Strawberry Pickers

Strawberry pickers bend in the fields
Outside Santa Barbara
Bent like harvesters in a painting by Millet
But these are not peasant farmers, these are not their fields
These hired hands, seasonal, migrant.

Vacant eyes, the outstretched hand—
Mural by Siqueiros 1932
Political refugee here in the land of bounty
Painted woman in rebozo
Almond-eyed, oval faced.
When the rifleman is unmasked—
Money bags at his feet
And the mouths of the dead stream blood.
J.P. Morgan on the opposite wall
From the soldier with the red star.

"The high cost of doing business"—
The coast that once was Mexico
Now is a border between water, land, and air,
The dock stretched out Pacificward
At night, fog obscures the stars
Night fishermen sink pots and lines
Out into ocean that breaks its own boundary.

La Brea

The little Thai-Chinese-Japanese joint in the strip mall
Has an altar above the cash register
All dripped gold flame pagoda
With real bananas (tiny ones)
Real slightly frayed carnations
Red lightbulb on a plastic candle
And electric incense sticks
That glow eternally and don't diminish
Into that reminder of impermanence—
Sweet smelling ash.

At the zoo:
peacocks
flamingos
polar bears
lorikeets
world's largest rodents
tiny deer of Asia
sea eagles, fisher cats
red panda, black rhinoceros
sun bears, langurs, lion tailed macaques
gazelles
and reindeer—the only deer
where the females also have antlers
kingfisher
otters

La Brea tar pits bubble in the park
Pleistocene, that era of extinction.
When the ocean receded
It left this sticky tar of asphalt
Sink hole to trap
The dire wolf, mastodon, the mammoth
Mother and child struggling in the pit.
giant ground sloth
saber-toothed cat
extinct camel
extinct western horse
Didn't you make a vow
To save all sentient beings?
The world was enormous then
Shaman in antlers
Out of Mongolia
Out of the Fourth World
One woman out of all the tribes
Drowned here, preserved as skeleton.
For who remains? Man,
Man and coyote, that scavenger . . .

San Luis Valley

The way I know this vast dry valley well
Is a sign of my life misspent
From Tres Piedras and Cozart's store
To San Antonio Mountain, free-standing monandnock
To the houses of Alamosa lit in the dark
Past Mosca, past Moffat, the turn-off to Saguache
To Salida with its lonely smelter tower of red brick
Its train tracks, its flower boxes
The questions it asks
About the heart . . .

It's not really possible
To look down on the past
Like a scale model of a railway
In which the train on the old mine grade
Passes the tiny sheep, the minuscule
Children playing outside the school
The 19th century courthouse
Architectural detail
Of scallop shells on a blue frieze
On a neglected second story.
It's not really possible
To arrange hope and desire
And with a flick of the switch
Let the model trains run through the snowy pass
And with another flick
Turn them off.

Still, it's tempting
To try and make sense
Of this landscape
Where my acquaintance is all with the insignificant
                                        and remote

A place like Kashgar, or Tashkent
Some place history tried to by-pass
And instead, where time got stuck.

Permian Reef

You might start at the top
Of the shale, and go down
Trying to find the start of the story—
Untidy life, preserved in stone.
A worm tube, a snail shell
What do they really tell
About the creature inside?
Darwin said the fossil record
Was like trying to read a book
With the pages torn out.
Alone, unhappy, and twenty-five
I read *Voyage of the Beagle*
In a successful attempt
To cheer myself up.
I don't truly understand
My own past
Let alone trilobites, the phyllopods
Preserved in limestone.
Or starting at the bottom
Working up, finding myself
Almost fifty, and on my desk
A piece of black polished stone
Marked by orthoceras
A squid with a hard conical shell
From the Saharan desert
Only 450 million years old.
These mountains were once reef
Beneath the sea

Not of coral, but built by sponges, algae.
Now desert of dry peaks, prickly pear
What once was—
Like the lungs of a great terrestrial beast—
A three-lobed sea . . .

Going East in West Texas

Weather balloon in UFO country
Takes on the shape of the mind,
Sky before sunset
Hawk, and
Mourning doves in the scattered leaves.
Yucca—Spanish Dagger—
Growing in the alkaline soil
Looks like a figure
Gesturing something
God must be listening
Without interference
Out on these plains.

In town, a snowman
Built of three tumbleweeds,
The bird that calls
Koo-koo-hoo, koo-koo-hoo . . .
What is it?
On the counter, there are cures:
Peppermint, iodine, gentian violet, castor oil.
The courthouse's Victorian cupola
Painted dark apricot, adorned
Like a Russian Easter egg;
Justice stands with her robe and scales
So high up
From below I can't tell
If her eyes are blind, or open . . .

The word GODBOLD on the grain elevator,
A two train night, and even more by morning.
Towards dawn, three men cross the yard
With their packs—who knows where they sleep—
Migrant labor.
Jerusalem Tree, rattle of dry seed pods,
The cactus which appears on the flag of Mexico,
Dragonflies, common iridescent skimmers
Those mosquito hawks, even here, far from water
Darting like thought,
Alone in a white room.

El Paso. Best Western

Freeway. White plastic bag
In wind.
Two startled pigeons.
Paperwhite narcissus
Blooming almost leafless
In hard bare soil.
No tanka. Polluted
Horizon. Mexico.
The moon over the parkinglot
3/4s moon.

In El Paso del Norte

In El Paso del Norte on the border
I woke crying and holding my own breasts
In a thin nightgown of black silk
As if I'd only just realized you were dead

The shabbos candles had burned out completely
In their makeshift holders of two motel water glasses
It's true, I was in love with someone else
In El Paso del Norte on the border

Two Postcards

MARFA, TEXAS. JANUARY, 2003

1. Untitled. Dan Flavin. 1996

Barracks glows from the corner—neon blue and green.
Coming on Stonehenge, wonder exists before the why.
Chaco has its sword of solstice light striking stone.
Even a barrow for the dead might suddenly admit daylight.
Mycenae has its beehive gate, Laos its plain of jars.
Huge structures exist, and not only in the mind.
This one is striped, alternating color theory.
What about those Manhattan glasses glowing in
$\qquad\qquad\qquad\qquad\qquad\qquad$ lounge windows
Or clef notes floating in neon
Or the red letters at the far end of town
Spelling CAFE against the darkness,
Behind these tubes of color
Which like all prison bars
Both restrict and liberate
We are as far away as God.

2. Eve of Saint John. Peter Hurd. 1960

Dark-haired girlchild stands out on the plains
Poised between dreams of women and the sky
Fifty miles west of Roswell, New Mexico
The sun is going down behind the mountains of San Patricio.
It is midsummer, time of bonfires at dusk

She holds a lit candle, as if trying
To read her future in the glow
In the far distance behind her
The house sheds light through each window like a dowry
A lone cowboy on a horse gallops by in a trail of dust.
In jeans and a thin white shirt, still breastless
She cups the flame
With a pensive look
As if a drop of wax revealed fortune.
I can't tell her much—as for me
Last night I laid these two postcards on my desk
Dreamed I was on a train
And heard a voice, speaking as if to me only, saying:
Every person in this world is lonely.

Notes on the Poems

p. 19   "Fabric"— "Spanish Work" is a kind of braided gold or silver thread. The technique was lost in the Holocaust. Thanks to the library at the Museum of International Folk Art for help with this poem.

p. 21   "Prayer Flag"—the notion of the past, present, and future tense of fire comes from Zen Master Dogen.

p. 59   "Homage to Mary Colter" and "La Posada. Winslow, Arizona"— Mary Colter, 1869-1910, was an architect, designer, and decorator for the Fred Harvey Company. Her integration of Native American styles resulted in the influences we still see today from Pueblo Deco to Santa Fe style. Her buildings mark the rim of the Grand Canyon, and include the Watchtower, influenced by the open towers of Anasazi ruins. She also built Hopi House there, based on the original pueblo.

p. 65   "Hundreds and Thousands"—all lines are direct quotes from the journals of Emily Carr. (1871-1945). She is probably western Canada's most famous painter of the period. She sought out remote villages and settlements and painted the totem poles she found there, forming the only record of much of this work. She is also a modernist, influenced by the European painters of the period. She was born, died, and lived most of her life in the city of Victoria on Vancouver Island, a provincial capital named for the Empress who is synonymous with the repression of the Victorian era, Empire, and paradoxically of female power.

p. 94   "Counting the Omer"—the Jewish calendar designates the 49 days between Passover and Succoth as the Omer. It is traditional to count each day with a blessing. I wrote a haiku per day during the Omer.

p. 103   "Paquimé"—this refers to the archeological site also called Casas Grandes in northern Mexico, which is connected to both Anasazi (Puebloan Ancestor) cities to the north and Aztecan ones to the south.

p. 107   "Cartography of Memory" was influenced by ideas in the book *The Inner Navigator* by Erik Jonsson.

p. 112   "Garment Industry" the description of animism is from *The Shaman's Coat: A Native History of Siberia* by Anna Reid.

Colophon

set in *Sabon*
—a typeface designed by Jan Tschichold & named
for Jacques Sabon, a Lyons typefounder who
inherited the original matrices of Claude Garamond.
In this rethinking of Garamond's face is the intention
that it work for all printing processes & reflects
the continuation of Tschichold's humane logic. It
elegantly merges Bauhaus sense of clean modernity
with Penguin regard for classic aesthetic.
In *The Form of the Book*, Tschichold wrote:
"Typography is both an art & science. Apparent
knowledge, based on what has been handed down
from one student to the next, like copies of copies
of flawed later editions (rather than the immediate
studying of the originals), does not bring anything
worthwhile . . . We have to return to the great
traditions of the Renaissance & the Baroque book,
study the originals & fill them with new life."

•

book design by J. Bryan

Miriam Sagan is author of more than a dozen books of poetry, fiction, and non-fiction. Her most recent include a memoir *Searching for a Mustard Seed: A Young Widow's Unconventional Story* (Quality Words in Print, 2003) and poetry *Archeology of Desire* (Red Hen, 2001); *The Widow's Coat* (Ahsahta Press, 1999); and *The Art of Love*, (La Alameda Press, 1994). She is also the author of  Dirty Laundry: *100 Days in a Zen Monastery*, (New World Library, 1999); *Unbroken Line: Writing in the Lineage of Poetry* (Sherman Asher, 1999); co-editor with Joan Logghe of *Another Desert: the Jewish Poetry of New Mexico* (Sherman Asher, 1998); and co-editor with Sharon Niederman of *New Mexico Poetry Renaissance* (Red Crane, 1994). Sagan is the poetry columnist for *Writer's Digest* and editor of the e-zine *Santa Fe Poetry Broadside*. (www.sfpoetry.org) She teaches on line for UCLA-Extension, Santa Fe Community College. Miriam Sagan lives in Santa Fe, New Mexico with her husband and daughter.